The Universe

Moons

Anne Welsbacher
ABDO & Daughters

Published by Abdo & Daughters, 4940 Viking Drive, Suite 622, Edina, Minnesota 55435.

Copyright © 1997 by Abdo Consulting Group, Inc., Pentagon Tower, P.O. Box 36036, Minneapolis, Minnesota 55435 USA. International copyrights reserved in all countries. No part of this book may be reproduced in any form without written permission from the publisher.

Printed in the United States.

Cover and Interior Photo credits: Peter Arnold, Inc.
Wide World Photos
Illustrations: Ben Dann Lander
Edited by Bob Italia

Library of Congress Cataloging-in-Publication Data

Welsbacher, Anne, 1955-
Moons / Anne Welsbacher.
    p.   cm. — (The universe)
Includes index.
Summary: Describes our moon, its size and physical features, as well as the moons circling other planets in our solar system.
ISBN 1-56239-721-4
1. Moon—Juvenile literature. [1. Moon. 2. Satellites.] I. Title. II. Series: Welsbacher, Anne, 1955-
Universe.
QB582.W45 1997
523.9'8—dc20   96-26775
                                                                          CIP
                                                                          AC

ABOUT THE AUTHOR
Anne Welsbacher is the director of publications for the Science Museum of Minnesota. She has written and edited science books and articles for children, and has written for national and regional publications on science, the environment, the arts, and other topics.

Contents

Many Moons in the Solar System 4

Earth's Moon 6

The Moons of Mars 8

The Jovian System 10

Saturn's Satellites 12

Saturn's Largest Moons 14

The Moons of Uranus 16

Neptune's Moons 18

Pluto's Charon 20

Moon Facts 22

Glossary 23

Index 24

Many Moons in the Solar System

The Sun is the center of the **Solar System**. Nine ball-shaped planets rotate around it. And smaller balls rotate around many of these planets. These smaller balls are called moons.

Earth's moon is called the Moon. Other planets have moons with different names, sizes, surfaces, and temperatures.

Earth and Pluto have one moon each. Mars has two moons. Neptune has eight moons.

Uranus has 15 moons. Jupiter has 16 moons. Saturn has 20 or more moons! Mercury and Venus have no moons at all.

Opposite page: A full moon rises over colorful carnival rides in a spectacular view.

Earth's Moon

The Moon is 240,000 miles (385,000 km) from Earth. About 30 Earths can fit between the Earth and the Moon.

The Moon is 2,160 miles (3,476 km) across. About four Moons would fit inside the Earth.

Like all moons, the Moon **orbits** a planet—our Earth. Light from the Sun reflects off half the Moon. Sometimes the Moon looks round. Other times it looks thin, like the edge of a pizza crust. These different **phases** depend on the Moon's position in its orbit.

The Moon has mountains, valleys, **craters**, and flat parts called **maria** (Latin for "seas"). The highest mountain is 30,000 feet (9,144 m) high—higher than Mount Everest, the tallest peak on Earth.

Because the Moon has no air, its sky is always dark—even when the Sun is shining. And when the sunlight shines on its surface, the Moon gets very hot—up to 215 degrees Fahrenheit (102 C). When it is dark, the surface can be very cold—as much as -243 Fahrenheit (-153 C).

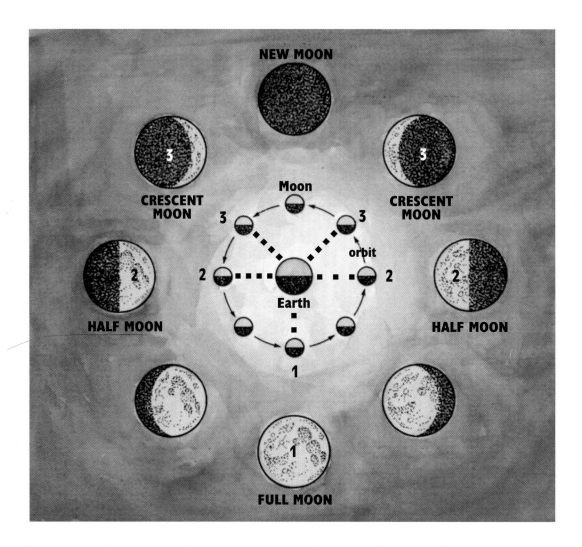

The phases of the Moon as they appear from Earth (outer diagram). The "shape" depends on the Moon's position in its orbit, and where the Sun and Earth are located (inner diagram). A full Moon (1) appears in the sky when the Earth is located between the Sun and the Moon. A half Moon (2) appears when the Moon and Earth are side-by-side. A crescent Moon (3) appears when the Moon is angled between the Earth and the Sun.

The Moons of Mars

Of all the inner planets (Mercury, Venus, Earth, and Mars), only Earth and Mars have moons.

Mars has two small, potato-shaped moons called Phobos (FOE-bus) and Deimos (DEE-mus). Phobos is about 14 miles (22 km) across and is covered with jagged **craters**. It **orbits** very close to Mars. Some **astronomers** believe it will one day fall to the Martian surface.

Deimos is only six miles (10 km) across and has smooth craters. It orbits farther away from Mars and is slowly moving away from the planet.

Opposite page:
Craters are found on most moons. When a meteorite (1) strikes the surface of a moon or planet, it causes an explosion (2), and leaves a crater (3).

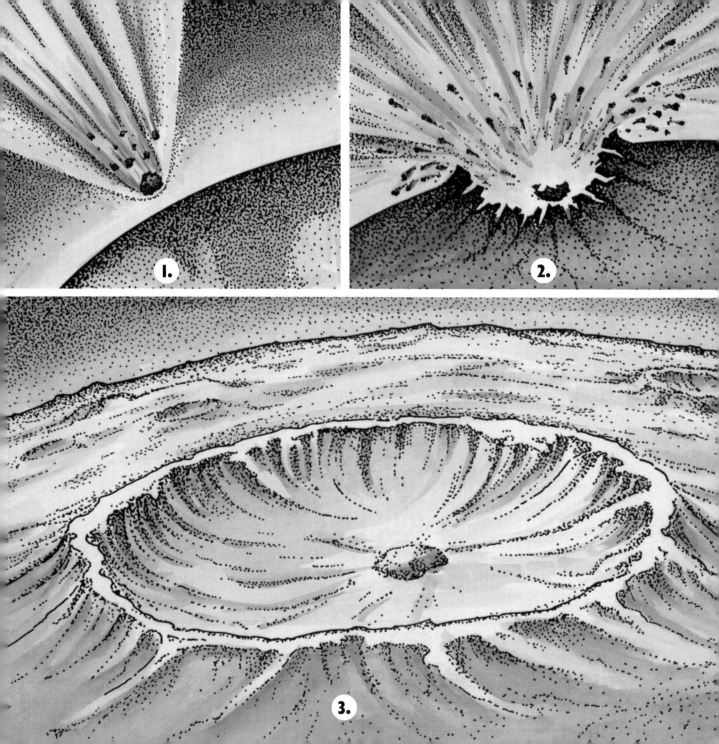

1.

2.

3.

The Jovian System

Jupiter and its 16 moons form a small "solar" system called the **Jovian System**.

Jupiter's four inner moons—Io (EYE-oh), Europa (yer-OH-pa), Ganymede (GAN-e-meed), and Callisto (kuh-LISS-toe)—are the largest. They are called the **Galilean** moons, named after the **astronomer** Galileo, who discovered them in 1610. They were the first moons, other than the Earth's, to be seen with a telescope.

The outer moons are much smaller. They probably were once **asteroids**. Jupiter's strong **gravity** may have pulled them into its **orbit**.

Io is closest to Jupiter. It is about the size of the Moon. It is reddish, and has active volcanoes. Europa has dark lines that zigzag its icy, smooth surface. Ganymede is Jupiter's biggest moon. Its icy crust is covered with grooves and **craters**.

Callisto is twice the size of the Moon. It also has a frozen surface. It formed about the same time as the planets—and much earlier than the other Jovian moons.

The planet Jupiter with two of its moons, Io (left and inset) and Europa.

Saturn's Satellites

Satellites are objects that **orbit** planets. Moons and rings are satellites.

Saturn has rings and at least 20 moons—more than any other planet in the **Solar System**. Included are seven large ones: Titan (TIE-tan), Mimas (MY-mus), Enceladus (en-suh-LAH-dus), Tethys (TETH-ez), Dione (DEE-on), Rhea (REE-uh), and Iapetus (eye-AP-e-tuss). Titan is the largest moon in the Solar System.

Saturn has thousands of rings made of ice particles. Some are as small as a fingernail. The largest are the size of a house.

Some of Saturn's outer moons are called **shepherd moons**. Shepherd moons keep the rings in orbit around Saturn.

Opposite page: Saturn and its moons.

Saturn's Largest Moons

Most of Saturn's large moons are covered with ice and **craters**. Enceladus has a surface of pure ice.

Titan is bigger than the planet Mercury. It is half rock and half ice.

Tethys has many craters. One is 10 miles (16 km) deep. Tethys also has a deep cut into one side. It might have broken open after being hit by a **meteorite** long ago.

Rhea has more craters than any of Saturn's moons. Tiny Mimas has a crater that covers one-third of its surface!

Dione shares an **orbit** with another moon called Dione B. They are the only moons in the **Solar System** to share an orbit.

Opposite page: Saturn's moon, Rhea, showing craters.

The Moons of Uranus

Most of Uranus' 15 moons are made of ice. Most have many **craters**. The five largest moons are Miranda (mur-AN-da), Ariel (AIR-e-ul), Umbriel (UM-bree-el), Titania (tie-TAN-e-ah), and Oberon (OH-bur-on).

Miranda is closest to Uranus and only 300 miles (483 km) across. It is covered with strange shapes and patterns. It has valleys, grooves, and cliffs higher than Earth's Grand Canyon.

Ariel and Umbriel are about the same size. Umbriel has craters. Ariel has valleys and canyons.

Oberon and Titania are the largest moons. They are about 1,000 miles (1,609 km) across, and have many craters. Oberon has a mountain 12 miles (19 km) high.

Uranus has a faint ring system. Some of the moons around Uranus are **shepherd moons**.

Uranus and its moons, from pictures taken by Voyager 2.

Neptune's Moons

Triton (TRY-ton) is the largest of Neptune's eight moons. Most moons **orbit** clockwise, or left to right, around a planet. Triton moves counter-clockwise, or right to left, around Neptune.

Triton also has **polar ice caps**. Its surface temperature is 400 degrees (F) below zero. It is the coldest body in the **Solar System**.

Nereid (NAR-eed) is Neptune's second-largest moon. The other six moons are dark and small. They are 30 to 300 miles (48 to 483 km) across.

Opposite page: An ice volcano on Neptune's moon, Triton. The black-and-white image near the center is thought to be the ice volcano that erupted, spewing ice particles and gas over a mile (2 km).

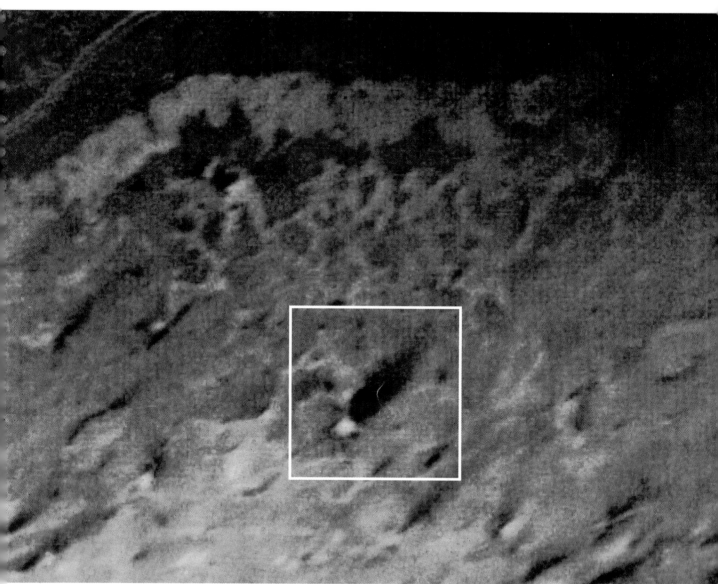

Pluto's Charon

Charon (SHARE-on), Pluto's only moon, is 750 miles (1,200 km) across—about half the size of Pluto. It is covered with ice.

Charon **orbits** close to Pluto and always faces the same side. It was discovered in 1978.

Some **astronomers** think Charon might have been a part of Pluto. A **meteorite** may have hit the planet and broke off a chunk. That chunk became Charon.

Opposite page: An illustration of Pluto's moon, Charon, as seen from Pluto.

Moon Facts

The time it takes the Moon
    to orbit the Earth...............................27 days, 7 hrs., 43 mins.

Planet with most moons ....Saturn (20 or more)

Largest moon..Titan (Saturn)

The only moon in the Solar System
    with an atmosphere...........................Titan (Saturn)

The largest moon compared
    to its planet ....Charon (Pluto)

Planets and Their Moons

Mercury.....................0

Venus 0

Earth 1

Mars 2

Jupiter 16

Saturn ....20+

Uranus 15

Neptune 8

Pluto...........................1

Glossary

asteroid (AS-ster-oyd)—very small planets that orbit the Sun, most of which are found between Mars and Jupiter.

astronomer (uh-STRAH-no-mer)—a scientist who studies outer space.

crater—a hole on the surface of planets and moons caused by collisions with meteorites.

Galilean (gal-uh-LEE-ann) **System**—the four largest moons circling Jupiter, named after the astronomer Galileo.

gravity (GRAV-uh-tee)—the natural force that causes objects to move toward the center of the Sun, Earth, or other heavenly bodies.

Jovian (JOE-vee-ann) **System**—Jupiter and its 16 moons.

maria (MAR-ee-uh)—the Latin word for "seas;" also, the large flat areas on the Moon.

meteorite (MEE-tee-er-rite)—a mass of rock or metal that strikes a planet.

orbit—the path that a moon or other satellite travels around a star or planet.

phase (FAZE)—the different "shapes" of the Moon.

polar caps—ice caps on the North and South poles of some planets and Neptune's moon, Triton.

shepherd (SHEP-erd) **moons**—moons that keep rings in place around their planets, named for shepherds who keep sheep from wandering away.

Solar System—Our Sun and all the things that orbit it, including the Earth, the Moon, and all the other planets.

Index

A

air 6
Ariel 16
asteroids 10
astronomers 8, 20

C

Callisto 10
canyons 16
Charon 20, 22
craters 6, 8, 10, 14, 16

D

Deimos 8
Dione 12, 14
Dione B 14

E

Earth 4, 6, 8, 10, 16, 22
Enceladus 12, 14
Europa 10

G

Galilean moons 10
Galileo 10
Ganymede 10
Grand Canyon 16
gravity 10

I

Iapetus 12
ice 12, 14, 16, 20

inner planets 8
Io 10

J

Jovian moons 10
Jovian System 10
Jupiter 4, 10, 22

M

maria 6
Mars 4, 8, 22
Mercury 4, 8, 14, 22
meteorite 14, 20
Mimas 12, 14
Miranda 16
Moon 6, 10
Mount Everest 6
mountains 6, 16

N

Neptune 4, 18, 22
Nereid 18

O

Oberon 16
orbit 6, 8, 10, 12, 14, 18, 20

P

phases 6
Phobos 8
planets 4, 6, 18, 22
Pluto 4, 20, 22
polar ice caps 18

R

Rhea 12, 14
ring system 16
rings 12

S

satellites 12
Saturn 4, 12, 14, 22
shepherd moons 12, 16
Solar System 4, 10, 12, 14, 18, 22
Sun 4, 6

T

telescope 10
Tethys 12, 14
Titan 12, 14, 16, 22
Titania 16
Triton 18

U

Umbriel 16
Uranus 4, 16, 22

V

valleys 6, 16
Venus 4, 8, 22
volcanoes 10